ISBN: 81-7436-095-6

Text:
Dr Bhagwan Dash
Suhasini Ramaswamy

Illustrations: Mariam Hasan, Amitabh
Photographs: Roli Collection, Lance Dane: pp. 24-25

Published by
© **Roli Books Pvt. Ltd. 2001**
Lustre Press Pvt. Ltd.
M-75 Greater Kailash, Part-II (Market)
New Delhi 110 048, India
Phone: 6442271, 6462782
Fax: 6467185
Email: roli@vsnl.com
Website: rolibooks.com
Conceived and designed
at Roli CAD Centre

Printed and bound at Singapore

indian
*aphrod**i**siacs*

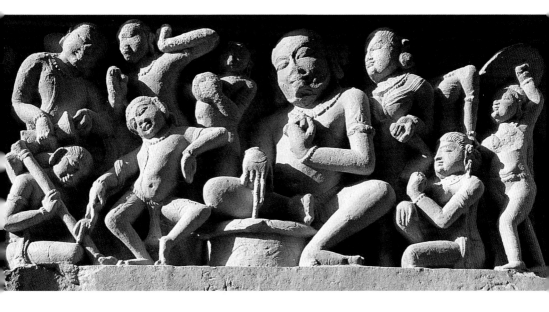

DR BHAGWAN DASH

SUHASINI RAMASWAMY

Lustre Press
Roli Books

While Manu, the law giver, stressed on procreation as the goal of sex, Vatsyayana emphasised on pleasure and enjoyment. Either way, Indian aphrodisiacs provide a fillip to a healthy sexual relationship.

con*t*ents

Sexual Fulfilment: Elixir for a Harmonious Life

*a*ncient Indian texts on Ayurveda, which is known as The Science of Life, have a direct and open approach to the study of sex in all its aspects. A great deal of importance is attached to sex and sexual activity as essential components for a harmonious relationship between a man and a woman within the bonds of marriage. While a physical relationship between a man and woman is meant to give pleasure to both, it is believed that this relationship was intended primarily for procreation. Physical satisfaction derived in the process of such activity should be for both partners, thus fostering a better mutual understanding. A sexually fulfiling relationship lays the foundation for harmony in the family and ultimately in society. Sexual fulfilment is deemed to be as essential as food and sleep for a complete and healthy life.

There are two main aspects of sexual activity and each complements the other. The first is the procreation of healthy children who carry on the lineage of the family and whose presence serves to bind both parents in a close familial relationship. Pleasure, the release of tensions and the bringing together of a man and a woman, physiologically, emotionally and intellectually constitute the other aspect. Both aspects call for compatibility between the partners; this enables them to fulfil their physical and emotional needs and in doing so, also fulfil their duties or right actions (*dharma*) or respective roles in their family. Such compatibility helps in ensuring that their marriage is a happy and lasting one and, in turn, affects their behaviour and contribution to society.

Arranged marriages continue to be the norm amongst many strata of Indian society, even though more and more young people today are selecting their

Physical gratification of both partners in a sexual relationship is extremely important.

own partners. Tradition demands that religion, caste, region and even sub-sects of communities are taken into consideration when looking for suitable matches. Among many Hindu families the matching of horoscopes is still the opening gambit when two families come together in a matrimonial alliance. In addition to height, complexion, educational qualifications and other attainments (for a girl); and qualifications, job, family status (for a boy), the matching of horoscopes gives the whole exercise a different dimension. The optimum number of excellent matching points is generally taken as eighteen when the horoscopes of a boy and a girl are compared. Among the important categories studied are caste (*varna*), clan (*gotra*), sub-sect, birth star (*tara*), the moon's position at the time of birth, the position of the planets, and such details as age and health. The pundit studies the temperament, psychological disposition

Indian texts highlight the importance of matching the horoscopes of the male and the female.

and intellectual ability of the individual to see whether the disposition is amiable (*vasya*) with that of the proposed spouse. He examines the pulse (*nadi*) which reveals the psychological hereditary factors; the constitution (*prakriti*) that is revealed by the status of the *dosas* or qualities or attributes which have characteristic effects on the body, and the predominance of one or more of them. The *doshas*: wind-*vata*, bile-*pitta* and phlegm-*kapha* are responsible for all bodily functions. As long as they are in a state of equilibrium in the body, the individual remains healthy. When one or more of the elements become unbalanced, there is morbidity and ill health. More important and relevant in the present context is the sexual compatibility of the boy and the girl.

The care and concern with which minute details are worked out in the mosaic of social and familial relationships only underline the importance that is attached to sex as an aspect of an individual's life.

Vatsyayana's *Kama Sutra* enjoins a man to choose a virgin of his own caste to be his wife and bear his children since society will accept only sons born of such a union as his legal heirs. Manu, the law giver, forbade the union of a high caste woman with a man of low caste. A man was prohibited from touching the wife of a relative, friend, high priest or king. Vatsyayana also describes the different kinds of women and their qualities: the *padmini* (lotus) woman is the epitome of womanly beauty; the *citrini* (like

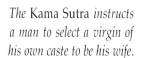
The Kama Sutra *instructs a man to select a virgin of his own caste to be his wife.*

*Vatsyayana categorises women as being slim and slender (**facing page**), demure (**top left**) or heavy, plump and highly sexed (**top right**).*

a picture) is full bosomed with a slender body; the *shankhini* (conch lady) is small, slim and demure; and the *hastini* (elephant woman) is heavy, plump and highly sexed. In aiming at compatibility, Vatsyayana recommends that men who are like the hare, the bull or the horse should match women whose physique matches that of the doe, the mare and the elephant, respectively. According to the sage Charaka, a person who is fortunate enough (because of his *karma* or actions in his past life) to get a woman of his liking benefits from it in terms of his physical and mental health—his complexion acquires a lustre and his other qualities blossom. 'She delights the heart; she is like Kama (the god of love); she bears similarity in her mental faculty with that of her husband; she is *vasya* (amiable); she is loved by her lover and with her excellent qualities she works like a noose of all the objects of senses.' (*Charaka: Chikitsa* 2:1:8-12)

Ayurvedic texts have devoted whole sections to therapies which include the use of drugs, diet and regimen essential for a sexually fulfilling and harmonious lifestyle. The *Charaka Samhita* is a supreme example of such a text which provides an insight into the importance of sexual activity and the place it had in ancient Indian thought. Depending on the times and sociological conditions prevailing, emphasis is given to the two major aspects of sex—procreation and enjoyment or pleasure. Manu, the stern law giver, stressed procreation as a goal; the sage Vatsyayana in his immortal classic, the *Kama Sutra,* showed greater concern for the enjoyment and pleasure derived from sex by both partners. Both, however, looked upon sexual activity as important in the life of an individual.

Just as sexual fulfilment is a *sine qua non* for harmonious living, one may even go so far as to say that the lack of such fulfilment can lead to disharmony and aberrations in the man-woman relationship resulting in discord within the family situation. Therefore, the role of sex and its proper understanding cannot be overemphasised.

Ayurvedic Teachings

The promotion of positive health and its maintenance through medical intervention constitutes one of the main goals of Ayurveda. It is towards this end that Ayurveda is divided into eight branches:

* *Kayachikitsa*-Internal medicine
* *Salya tantra*-Surgery
* *Shalakya tantra*-Management of diseases specific to the head and neck
* *Agada tantra*-Toxicology
* *Bhuta vidya*-Psychiatry
* *Kaumara bhrtya* or Pediatrics including Midwifery
* *Rasayana*-the Science of Rejuvenation
* *Vajikarana*-the Science of Aphrodisiacs

Maintenance therapy is advised for those who are healthy in order to help them retain their health status. Curative measures through medical intervention are meant for those whose health is impaired so that they can become healthy. Health in this context includes mental tranquility and spirituality which are important for physical well-being since the mind exercises great influence over the body. Spirituality also provides the direction for righteous conduct. The promotion of healthy sex and the dissemination of the right kind of information in this respect is of immense importance to lay the ground rules for a healthy society. While Indian texts prescribe certain codes of conduct in the practice of sex, the focus is always the individual-in-society, beginning at the family level.

The Western attitude towards sex does not subscribe to the views expressed in Indian texts. With the changing social mores, sexual relationships have acquired a different meaning. Procreation is not considered a major factor in this relationship any longer.

Indian texts lay down certain codes of conduct in sexual practice.

In Europe and in many other parts of the Western world, marriage is not always the norm between a man and a woman. The family as a social institution is breaking up and, as a consequence, relationships are not always stable. Divorce, extramarital relationships and a lack of mutual understanding between partners are some of the causes that lead to frustration and social problems.

Juxtaposed with the above is the empirical and pragmatic outlook found in Indian thought as it unfolds itself from the extant texts of Charaka, Vagabhata, Sushruta and Vatsyayana, to name only a few. Primarily speaking, sex and procreation go together; sex is not merely a pleasurable pastime between two human beings in a fleeting relationship. Sex is a dynamic process that brings

The relationship between a man and a woman should be a bonding of bodies, minds and intellects.

man and woman together in an intimate and lasting relationship. It is a bond between two bodies, minds and intellects. It is not simply a physical relationship where problems can be treated with quick-fix solutions, such as drugs, implants or other means. Western medicine has its limitations which can be assessed only in relation to what was established centuries ago in ancient Indian texts. There is hardly any aspect of sexuality that has not been studied by the ancients. The bases for such studies are varied, as for example: psychosomatic, dietetic, overindulgence in sex, sexually transmitted diseases, injuries, the practice of celibacy, congenital problems, aging—to name but a few. Even semen has been categorised in order to identify abnormalities and afflictions. Likewise, impotence, one of the most common afflictions, has been classified along with other sexual disorders. Indian texts clearly lay down a sexual code in which prominence is given to the ages of the partners in sexual activity, the persona involved, the time, the place, frequency, season and other factors.

Medical intervention in the form of *rasayana* and *vajikarana* therapies is an aid towards sexual fulfilment. *Rasayana* is a rejuvenating and nourishing therapy which involves the observance of a strict diet and self-imposed discipline as regards the practice of sex. The body and the mind are cleansed thoroughly during this vigorously administered therapy so as to make the individual receptive for the *vajikarana* or aphrodisiac therapy which is to follow.

The care and meticulous attention to detail that is given in describing the working of these therapies only goes to show the seriousness and the importance that the ancients attached to sexual activity as part of an individual's life. Despite the use of aphrodisiacs and other suggestions, the practice of sex is not always successful. Sexual fulfilment is elusive at times and the causes need to be studied.

A 1999 *Readers' Digest* publication brought together several family stories about couples and counsellors, providing answers to pressing questions such as: What do men and women want from a marriage? How can one bring back fun in a marriage? How can marital problems be solved? The titles to some of the stories are revealing: "How to Read your Partner's Sex Signals"; "Five Sex Secrets Women Wish Husbands Knew"; "Why Are We Not Having More Fun in Bed?"; "How to Maintain an Erotic Marriage", and several others in the same vein.

The answers to these questions and to many more can be found in ancient Indian texts. To understand them in their own framework and to identify their relevance to contemporary situations and problems arising out of them, is a worthwhile effort.

The Indian
View of Sex

*i*ndian thought as embodied in the ancient texts — *Sastras, Srutis, Smritis, Sutras, Puranas* is an integrated system which is based on a single framework which gives it a uniquely holistic character. Any book of divine or recognised authority, especially a law book such as the *Dharma Sastra* or Code of Laws is known as a *Sastra*. Thus there is the *Shilpa Sastra*—a science of mechanics which also includes sculpture and architecture; the *Artha Sastra* by the celebrated author Kautilya which is devoted to economics and polity; the *Natya Sastra*, the treatise on theatre and dance; and the *Kama Sastra*—the art of love. The *Smritis* (recall of ancient wisdom) handed down by tradition are distinguishable from the *Srutis* which came from direct revelation. *Sutras* are rules or aphorisms—verses expressed in brief and technical language relating to rituals or rites. The best examples of the *Sutras* are the *Yoga Sutra* of the sage Patanjali and the even more widely-known treatise on love—the celebrated *Kama Sutra* by the seer Vatsyayana. The *Sutras* date back to the sixth century B.C.

The *Puranas* contain ancient legends about gods and goddesses relating to the creation of the universe, its destruction and renovation; the genealogy of gods and patriarchs; the reigns of the *manus* or mythological progenitors of mankind and the history of the solar and lunar races of kings. The *Vishnupurana* is the best example of this genre. The epics of the *Ramayana* and the *Mahabharata* fall under what is known as *itihaasa*–legendary poems about legendary heroes.

Taken together the entire body of Indian thought is concerned with the

The Sastras, Srutis, Smritis, Sutras *and* Puranas *are texts that embody Indian thought and legends.*

individual in society and in his total environment. The legends and stories serve to illustrate the precepts of a good life which can be emulated along with the pitfalls which need to be avoided.

Guiding Principles for a Righteous Life: Purusharthas

The principles on which life can be lived without straying away from the righteous path and which provide guidance are known as the *purusharthas:* righteous conduct (*dharma*), economic gain (*artha*), desire and love (*kama*) and finally, salvation (*moksa*). Righteous conduct guides the individual towards his role in relationship to his environment. Environment here encompasses the individual's entire universe consisting of the animate and the inanimate and the individual's place in his or her family and society. Righteous conduct provides the guiding principles of the role of a father towards his family – his wife and children; that of a king in looking after his subjects and working for their good before his own and that of his family. It outlines the role of a physician in taking care of the health of his patients and healing their ailments. Righteous conduct advises patients to pay for treatment received. However, it also states that the doctor should not put economic gain before righteous conduct.

Human nature being what it is, economic gain and desire are the main principles that motivate the individual towards fulfilling his goals. But they should never take precedence over righteous conduct.

The ultimate goal can be expressed as salvation or *moksha*. In this journey towards the ultimate goal the individual is guided from birth to death and even beyond death by a series of what are known as rites of passage (*samskaras*) which make the transition from one stage to the next as smooth as possible.

The cycle of events from birth to death and beyond begins with the birth of the child and the cleansing of the newborn or *jatakarma*. The throat and palate are cleaned of unctuous substances, as is the body. On the tenth day after the child's birth, the mother and child are massaged with oil and given a warm bath. The naming ceremony or *namakarana* takes place with the parents giving the child a name. Parenthood is ritually established with the priest, family and friends in attendance. This is a time for feasting and rejoicing, more so if the child is a boy. Indian thought regards the family as an institution that evolves through generations through a succession of male heirs. Six months after the child's birth, before the milk teeth begin to appear, the child has his first meal of cooked rice – this is yet another occasion for more rituals and more feasting for the family and friends. This ceremony is known as the *annaprashana* ceremony. At the end of one year, the first birthday or *abdapurthi* is celebrated with great joy. The important occasion following the completion of one year and before the thread ceremony or *upanayana,* which is either in the seventh, ninth or eleventh year when the boy is prepared for the life of a celibate (*brahmacharya*), is the first tonsure or *coula.*

Puberty is a momentous occasion in the life of a girl. She is made to have a ritual bath, after which she is bedecked with finery.

Puberty is another such threshold for a girl. Even today, among some communities in south India, this occasion is celebrated with a great deal of publicity. Friends and relatives shower gifts on the girl. On the fourth day after the beginning of the menstrual cycle, the girl is made to have a ritual bath and wear new clothes; she is bedecked with flowers and jewellery and a feast is laid on. The astrologer studies the time, the day and the star under which the menstrual cycle begins and there is rejoicing if everything is considered auspicious by him; in fact the astrologer's calculations determine the girl's future as a wife and mother.

The rite of the sacred thread ceremony or *upanayana* for the boy is in preparation for his life as a celibate student. The onset of adolescence with the accompanying changes in the body and mind of the student are recognised and the code of conduct is outlined so that the period when learning is to be assimilated, is utilised without any distractions. Emphasis is given to the beliefs that the body is still maturing, the body tissues are not yet fully strengthened and the mind is yet to mature. Sex before twenty-five years is prohibited for this reason. Celibacy and the focus of the mind on the acquisition of knowledge are the attributes favoured for the celibate.

Four Stages in the Life of Man

Life as a celibate or *brahmacharya* marks the first stage or *ashrama* of an individual existence. With childhood being left behind and adulthood and marriage in the distance, *brahmacharya* is the transitory stage of a celibate. The system of *gurukulas* or places where the disciples of a guru lived and studied together under his guidance provided the ambience for acquiring knowledge to the exclusion of everything else. Legend has it that at one such *gurukula* a young student was so entirely wrapped up in his studies that he did not even notice that a spoonful of castor oil was being served in his rice every day instead of clarified butter (*ghee*). Months later, when he suddenly became aware of it, he questioned the sage's wife about the substitution. The guru decided then and there that the young man's student days were over.

The next stage or *ashrama* in an individual's life is the life of a householder or *grihasthashrama*. The body and the mind having attained maturity, the individual is ready to shoulder the responsibility of a marital relationship. Sex and procreation are central to this stage of life. Even while extolling the virtues of celibacy and sainthood, Indian thought bestows a unique status on this stage in an individual's life. Vagabhata described it thus: 'We approve *brahmacharya* -

~

The life of a householder or **grihasthashrama** *is the second stage in a man's life when he is ready to shoulder the responsibility of a wife and family.*

~

celibacy, which is the cause of righteousness, success in life, long life, good for both the worlds/lives (the present and future lives) and always pure.' (*Ashtanga Hridaya: Uttara* 40:4). He also stated that a man without children was like a tree without shade, which bore foul-smelling flowers, did not have branches, and did not bear fruit. It stood alone.

The life of a householder or *grihasthi* is thought of as the most complete and fulfiling stage in an individual's life. The place of sex and sexual activity is taken cognizance of as a part of the individual's life just as drinking, eating and sleeping. Man's instinctive desire is to extend the family, the clan and then the race. The desire for progeny or *putraisana* finds mention in the *Upanishads* as a primeval instinct of mankind. Thus sexual intercourse and the act of procreation have been under intensive study for more than two thousand years in India. Far from being taboo or kept under wraps, discussion about sex has been frank, open and uninhibited. Temple sculpture, such as that in Khajuraho and Konaraka, and miniature paintings of various schools are fairly explicit in their portrayal of sexual postures.

There is an interesting story told and retold through the centuries about the great celibate saint and founder of the school of Indian philosophy known as *Advaita* or non-dualism. Adi Sankaracharya who was a celibate or *bala brahmachari* had a short lifespan of only 32 years. The great saint and teacher often sought out leaders of other schools in order to engage them in debate. On one such occasion Sankara was directed to Visvarupa, a disciple of Kumarila Batta, a great teacher and the foremost proponent of the philosophy of *Purva Mimamsa*. (This philosophy, in brief, discusses the ritual part of the scriptures and deals with the means of attaining Brahman (salvation) as opposed to *Advaita* which states that all reality has to be understood in terms of the empirical and the transcendental.)

However, to continue with the story, Visvarupa is sometimes identified with the great sage Mandana Misra whose wife was also said to be very learned. A unique debate ensued between the two great philosophers which lasted for several weeks. Even more unique was the fact that the referee was none other than Bharati, Sage Visvarupa's wife who was regarded as an incarnation of the goddess Saraswati herself, so well versed was she in the *Vedas* and the *Upanishads*. At stake here was a whole way of life; the loser was to abandon his calling and become the disciple of the other. If Sankara won, Visvarupa would have to renounce the world, his wife, wealth and other possessions in order to become a celibate, mendicant or *sanyasi*. On the other hand, victory for Visvarupa meant that Adi Sankara would consent to get married and become a *grihasthi* or householder. In the end, Visvarupa had to concede defeat to the powerful arguments of Sankara. Bharati was an extremely fair judge but before declaring her final verdict, she threw a challenge to her husband's protagonist, Sankara. She asked him questions about *Kama sastra* (the science of love). Sankara who had renounced the world at a very young age, had never experienced love or sex. He therefore asked for some time before he could take up her challenge. Within the given time and with the help of his yogic powers, he entered the body of a dying king and experienced the art of love with his queen. On returning to Visvarupa's home he was able to answer all Bharati's questions to her satisfaction and finally won the debate. As agreed upon, Visvarupa was ordained a *sanyasi* and took the name of Suresvara, thus becoming the most celebrated of Sankara's disciples. The point of emphasis here is the importance given to the experience of the householder with his knowledge of desire (*kama*). Visvarupa, it must be noted, was also accepted as Suresvara the *sanyasi* after having been a householder and husband of the learned Bharati.

As in all other fields, the parameters set for leading a good life are universal and only need application in order to understand and realise their full benefits. In placing sex and the man-woman relationship within the framework of the stages of life or *ashramas* subject to the guiding principles of the *purusharthas,* Indian thought recognises the significance of such a relationship and its place in an individual's journey through life.

~

There are several rituals laid down in the married life of a couple which transform the celibate into a householder.

~

24

Texts such as the Charaka Samhita *maintain that rejuvenation treatment* (rasayana) *should be carried out before aphrodisiac therapy* (vajikarana).

The first night spent by the couple is traditionally celebrated with song and dance.

Marriage and the rituals accompanying it are called the *samskaras* which transform the celibate into a householder. The first night spent together by the bride and the groom is traditionally celebrated with song and friendly advice on both sides. The bridal chamber is decorated with flowers and the fragrance of flowers and incense fills the air. Sweets made specially for the occasion are kept at the bedside along with a jar of warm milk. Milk, according to Ayurveda, is an excellent vitaliser and should be taken before and after sexual activity. Milk plays an important role in aphrodisiac or *vajikarana* therapy.

Pumsavana karma is one of the rituals performed during pregnancy. The ritual is performed for the welfare of the foetus and the mother during the second month. If the rites are performed correctly, they can even help to change the sex of the child. These rites are still performed among certain communities during the sixth or eighth month of pregnancy. The husband and wife offer prayers to all the gods and goddesses to bless the pregnant woman and the child that is to be born. The juice of certain herbs is squeezed into the nostrils of the pregnant woman by the husband; this is supposed to determine the sex of the progeny and provide strength to the foetus growing in her womb.

Sexual functioning is not merely an expression for reproduction and gender identity. In the course of sexual activity, the emotional bond between the partners is cemented. In this context, texts such as *Charaka Samhita,*

Ashtanga-hrdaya and *Sushruta Samhita,* among others, lay stress on the use of aphrodisiacs. It is towards this end that promotive treatment (*rasayana*) and aphrodisiac therapy (*vajikarana*) are recommended.

Charaka lays emphasis on *rasayana* as a necessary prelude to the administration of the *vajikarana* therapy or the use of aphrodisiacs. *Rasayana* is a rejuvenation therapy which should precede *vajikarana*. The latter therapy can be applied only on a healthy individual. *Rasayana* is the science of nutrition and it is classified into three kinds: *ajasrika, kamya* and *naimittika. Ajasrika rasayana,* for example, calls for continued consumption of milk, clarified butter (*ghee*) and other such nutritious foods so that the optimum nutrition is maintained by direct nourishment. *Rasayana* as a programme of nourishment, also lays down certain restrictions on diet, physical activity and other factors. *Vajikarana* therapy or aphrodisiac therapy, on the other hand, comprises the release of restrictions and the stimulation of the sexual urge through the use of aphrodisiacs. *Vajikarana* is advised after *rasayana* in order to help promote the natural instinct for sex at the right time so that conception is by choice, not by accident. Both therapies, it must be noted, are to be used on persons who are healthy and not ill or diseased. *Rasayana* aims to nourish the tissues (*dhatus*) and *vajikarana* aims to release the nourished *dhatus* at the appropriate time, thus ensuring normal and healthy progeny. *Vajikarana* is not considered a means to increase sexual pleasure alone – this is not in tune with the tenets of Ayurveda. The individual who chooses to go in for *vajikarana* should be able to practise self-control. The application of *vajikarana* by one who lacks self-control is harmful to the family and to society. The user turns out to be an anti-social element. *Vajikarana* therapy benefits the male rather than the female since the male tissues are used more in sexual intercourse.

Ayurvedic texts are also clear about the physiological age groups between which sexual activity should take place. Persons below twenty-five years and above seventy years are not deemed fit for such activity. Pre-adolescent sex causes loss of strength and vigour in the male since the male sexual glands and neuro-endocrines have not completely matured at this stage. Sexual activity is not advisable after seventy years as there is loss of natural vitality and strength. According to Sushruta, at the time of marriage, the male should be above twenty-five years old, while the female should have crossed sixteen years of age.

Ayurvedic texts have studied sex so thoroughly that there is scarcely any aspect which has not been included in the Do's and Don'ts of sexual activity.

Desire and pleasure are influenced by the seasons, time and place, constitution, age and other factors relating to the partners.

These aspects include the seasons, the time, the place, the constitution or *prakriti* of the partners, the age, the psyche, sleep, rest, sexo-pathology and morbid states. Many scattered references in Ayurvedic literature also indicate a sexual code of conduct. Apart from age, sex with the wife of an enemy, friend, guru or student or with a *sanyasin* (a celibate nun) or an old lady is prohibited. The female partner is not to be looked upon exclusively as an object of recreation. Partners should not be changed in an irresponsible manner. The list is quite exhaustive....

Not all men who are physically strong are capable of procreation or fathering progeny. A hefty and strong man may be weak when having intercourse with a woman. On the other hand, a physically lean and thin male may be capable of satisfactory intercourse and may have numerous children.

The *Kama Sutra* explores the human psyche and the emotions that govern human behaviour. A treatise on love, it comprises aphorisms on desire and pleasure. Contrary to general belief, only one of the sections deals with the techniques of physical love-making. The others cover topics such as decoration of the house, creating an ambience for practising the art of love, advice on how to woo a bride, suggestions on how husbands and wives should behave with one another, how to celebrate religious festivals, and so on. Basically speaking, the *Kama Sutra* is one of the earliest attempts to define a man-woman relationship. Vatsyayana's keen observation and understanding of the nuances of this relationship and his emphatic assertion that both man and woman must derive pleasure from the art of love-making impart a universality to his aphorisms and their relevance remains even today. Human nature continues to be the same. Human psychology and physiology have not altered a whit since the sage Vatsyayana wrote his magnificent work on love.

Sterility and Impotence

a constantly recurring theme in Indian thought is the Guiding Principles or *purusharthas* and their universal relevance. The benefits of having children are stressed time and again. An individual gets the benefits of righteousness (*dharma*), wealth, economic gains (*artha*), love (*priti*) and fame (*yasas*) through his/her progeny. The objective of sexual intercourse, apart from momentary pleasure, is procreation (which translated as 'begetting sons' in the context of those times). Aphrodisiac therapy (*vajikarana*) is highly recommended so that this purpose can be fulfilled.

> The child with his faltering gait, incomprehensible speech, dust-covered body and saliva-smeared face is gladdening to the heart; which other thing is equal to it in its sight and touch? Which is equal to it in enhancing the reputation, righteousness, prestige, wealth, dignity and lineage of the family?
>
> *Astanga-hrdaya: Uttara* 40:10-11

Sterility and impotence are major problems which cause rifts in a man-woman relationship and strike at the roots of a harmonious family life. Fertility clinics have mushroomed all over urban areas and impotence therapy has acquired a status as a field of specialisation. In fact, the International Society for Impotence Research held its seventh World Meeting in San Francisco, USA, in November 1996. The treatment of impotence, the commonest of sexual problems, has run the entire gamut from psychoanalysis to implant surgery to gene therapy.

Impotence is a major sexual problem which needs to be addressed.

Psychologists, sexologists and andrologists have now given way to a new breed of medicine men – the gene therapists.

Judging by the number of magazines and books that have proliferated on sex and sexual problems, there appears to be an increasing demand for literature of this genre. Health magazines and clinical journals are devoted mostly to discussions on sex-related problems. Under cover of anonymity, endless questions are asked by male and female readers alike regarding the physical condition of reproductive organs; psychological doubts and anxieties are voiced about infertility, incapacity to perform, imagined and real ailments, and many more sexually related problems. Being an important aspect of the individual's well-being, it is essential that the information disseminated is of the right kind and that it is easily accessible to those who are in need of it. Modern medicine tends to deal with the subject of sex mainly at the physical level with tentative forays into the psychological, where one impinges on the other. Modern medicine, however, has its limitations when compared to the holistic nature of the Indian system with its accent on the maintenance of positive health and prevention of disease. There is more and more evidence to show that Modern medicine does not have the final say in matters of sexual activity. The Indian system of Ayurveda has a vast treasure-house of therapies and drugs relating to the topic. Understanding its complexity and adapting it to today's needs will be an extremely rewarding exercise.

~

Freud's claim that most male sexual problems were due to deeply repressed psychological factors was challenged by a biologist who attributed them to a defective male organ.

~

For Freudian scientists at the beginning of the twentieth century, sexuality was all in the head. Towards the end of the century, a molecular biologist attributed it to a defective male sexual organ. Psychopathy assumed that in almost all cases of sexual problems, particularly impotence, deeply repressed, unresolved and unconscious conflicts were the cause. Psycho-analysis was used as a tool to resolve such conflicts as it was believed that a uniform sexual response was the result of a uniform childhood experience. The Kinsey Report did not, however, subscribe to this view. This report was a pioneering piece of work with a modern scientific approach to the study of sex. In the sixties Mrs Virginia Johnson and Dr William Masters conducted laboratory research on human sexual response and human sexual inadequacy. They created special packages of sexual training programmes. Johnson and Masters integrated behavioural training and psycho-education but their programmes were too extended and required a somewhat longish period without intercourse. There were also other difficulties that made the programmes inoperable.

Today there are three major approaches to sexual problems: the *psychological* which aims at resolving psycho-sexual conflicts and marital relationships; the *behavioural* approach which focuses on pleasure-giving

Sexual desire can cease if the partner is not of one's choice. In such cases, the centre in the brain which issues instructions to the mind, refuses to get activated.

techniques; and *physical therapies* using non-invasive vacuum devices, invasive and painful injections of vasodilator drugs as well as surgery – vascular and implant. Other medications are still on trial. The widely acclaimed miracle drug Viagra (Sildenafil) has also proved to be effective only in certain cases. It is contraindicated in patients with heart ailments. More important, it does not arouse sexual desire. There are also other aphrodisiacs such as cantharides made from dried beetles which are widely touted as effective but have been found to be particularly harmful. They are said to cause irritation in the urinary and the genital tracts and can also cause infection, scarring and a burning sensation in the mouth and throat. Modern medicine is still in an experimental stage when it comes to aphrodisiacs.

What Leads to Sexual Inadequacies?

Ancient Indian Ayurvedic texts, on the other hand, contain the results of innumerable studies related to sexual inadequacies and their causes, both physical and emotive. The *Sushruta Samhita* elaborates on impotence and analyses the causes of sexual inadequacies into seven categories:

❖ *Psychosomatic factors:* Sexual desire can cease owing to bitter thoughts, anger and similar feelings. Not getting the partner of one's choice or being forced to engage in sex against one's wishes are also circumstances which cause impotence. Suppression of sexual desire is another. The mind plays a prominent role in any kind of sexual activity. The centre in the brain which issues commands has to be activated. Yoga and other regimen can play a useful role in enhancing and regulating sexual activity.

❖ *Dietetic factors:* Excessive consumption of foods which by nature are acidic, salty, pungent or heat producing in the Ayurvedic sense of the term, can dry up the watering principle of the organism or *saumya dhatu* and cause impotence.

❖ *Over-indulgence in sex:* Virile impotence can be caused by over-indulgence in sex or sexual addiction by those who are exhausted or aging or promiscuous and do not resort to the use of suitable aphrodisiacs.

❖ *Sexually transmitted diseases:* Diseases such as syphillis which affect the male generative organ and other injuries which destroy the spermatic chord decimate the power of coition altogether.

Andropause among men can lead to a slackening interest in sex.

❖ *Celibacy:* The practice of celibacy and the constant suppression of the sexual urge by those who believe in austerity can result in permanent damage of the semen-producing organs in the body.

❖ *Congenital defects:* Impotence can be caused by congenital defects such as the absence, malfunction or retarded growth of the internal genitalia.

❖ *Middle and old age:* Menopause among women and similarly, andropause among men can lead to a slackening of interest in sex. Also, those above seventy years of age experience a definite weakness in semen (*sukra*) production.

The *Charaka Samhita* talks of four kinds of impotence, which is generally applicable to erectile dysfunction.

❖ Decrease in the sperm count (*bijopaghata-janya*): Impotence of this kind may be due to a diet which is cold, dry and made from incompatible recipes; nutritional deficiencies; suppression of hunger and exertion.

❖ Deformity in the sexual organs (*dhvajopaghata-janya*): Impotence can also be caused by excessive indulgence in masturbation, perverted sex, intercourse with a diseased female, sexual intercourse with a female during her periods and injurious local applications which can lead to structural deformity in the sex organs.

❖ Old age (*vruddhavastha-janya*): Vital tissues age and the body becomes deficient in essential hormones. There may also be functional abnormalities of the senso-motor organs; suppression of hunger and overexertion could lead to general debility. All these could be causative factors for impotence after the age of fifty.

❖ Emotional problems (*shukrakshaya-janya*): Impotence can also be borne out of constant exposure to debilitating physical or mental circumstances such as continuous anxieties, mental tension, sorrow or trauma; jealousy, anger or hyper-excitement. The loss of vitality and functional impotence can cause severe immunodeficiency and even result in death.

There is a fifth category of impotence which is due to genetic factors and is, therefore, irreversible. This is known as Impotence from birth (*janmajata klaibya*).

Charaka also describes various abnormalities in the semen which can lead to infertility. Treatment for these can be found in medicinal herbs which help restore the normal constitution (*sodana*). Replenishing remedies (*santarpana*) and various therapies or *rasayanas* modulate immunity and help check the anti-immune processes. Gynaecological diseases (*yoni rogas*) can also be treated by aphrodisiac therapies or *vajikarana*.

Only semen with certain qualities of colour, taste, smell, consistency, touch and quantity and which passes through the urethra leaving no burning sensation, is capable of procreation. Defective semen either prevents conception and even if conception does take place, it results in offspring with defects. The semen or *sukra* is said to consist of sperm (literally, seeds) or *bijas*. Each sperm is again composed of parts or *bijabhagas* which are responsible for the creation of different organs and viscera of the body. These parts have sub-parts or *avayavas* which, if afflicted, can lead to structural and functional defects in the corresponding organs in the body of the foetus. (The modern concept of chromosomes and genes appears similar to this age-old ayurvedic concept of *bijabhaga* and *bijabhagavayava*).

Any deviation from total health or morbidity manifests itself in negative effects on the individual's sexuality. It can result in disinterest and even aversion to females and to sex. Haematological and hepatobiliary disorders can cause loss of vital strength, lassitude and disinterest in sex. Haemorrhoids and other such disorders can also pose problems, while diabetes and obesity can have a negative impact on sexual performance. Likewise erectile dysfunctions and premature ejaculation can hamper sexuality. Ayurveda teachers (*acharyas*) affirm the influence and importance of the female from the point of erection to the end – the process of the formation of the zygote in the uterus. Most disorders, including impotence, are common in the male and are often transmitted to the foetus by the male.

In women, lack and loss of sexual desire is known as frigidity. There can also be sexual aversion and lack of sexual enjoyment. Women can fail to respond to sexual arousal. On the other hand there can be excessive sexual desire too. Vaginal dryness, pain during intercourse, difficulty or vaginismus as well as orgasmic dysfunction are problems relating to women.

Aphrodisiac therapies, if followed properly, can provide solutions to most of these problems. All this calls for a change in lifestyle.

Types of Aphrodisiacs

*i*n order to understand the role of aphrodisiacs in therapies, it is necessary to explain the role that promotive treatment (*rasayana*) and aphrodisiac therapy (*vajikarana*) play in Ayurveda. The significance of these two branches of Ayurveda has not diminished even though the change in lifestyle has been great since the times of Charaka and Sushruta.

Rasayana being a promotive treatment and *Vajikarana* an aphrodisiac therapy, the aim of both is to promote and enhance the health of the individual in order to live a fulfilling life regulated by certain guiding principles or *purusharthas:* righteous action (*dharma*), economic gain (*artha*) and desire (*kama*).

Rasayana therapies aim at improving cells, organs and systems in the individual that have actual or anticipated vulnerability. The goal in *rasayana* is to ensure that the tissues are endowed with good and indeed the best qualities so as to pre-empt any risk to them. Such a programme can only be undertaken after the individual attains maturity. As mentioned earlier, an immature child indulging in sex acts will become a prey to morbidity. Likewise an old man over seventy is likely to break down after a sex act. The condition of an old man over seventy years is likened to a dry brittle piece of wood eaten away by insects, which disintegrates on touch.

The therapeutic effects of *rasayana* and *vajikarana* can benefit those who have attained maturity, who have self-control, whose minds do not dwell on evil thoughts, are free from anger, hatred and other negative qualities, and who wish to pursue righteousness (*dharma*) as a way of life in fulfilment of their duties.

Aphrodisiac recipes should be administered after purifying the body and considering one's strength.
(Astanga-hrdaya: Uttara: 40:12a)

Rasayana and *vajikarana* can be administered only to healthy individuals. *Rasayana* precedes *vajikarana* and prepares the individual for *vajikarana*. *Rasayana* too can only be given as a therapy to healthy individuals. Diseases and ailments must be cured even before *rasayana* is undertaken as this rejuvenation therapy calls for a good deal of self-discipline and a strict dietary regimen. Both the mind and body are subjected to a thorough cleansing before the nourishing therapy is administered.

Individuals who are willing to undergo the rigours of a disciplined life must first subject themselves to *rasayana* therapies which will help cleanse their minds and bodies of harmful, unwanted thoughts, body toxins and generally tone up the entire system in readiness to receive *vajikarana* or aphrodisiac therapy. *Vajikarana* therapy will enable such individuals to enjoy the pleasures of sex and procreate children endowed with intelligence, keenness of intellect, good health, strength and vigour and thus ensure fitness of mind and body in future generations.

Rasayana: Promotive Treatment

Charaka's chapter on promotive treatment or *rasayana* is divided into four quarters, each quarter dealing with promotive treatment based on certain drugs or combinations of drugs which are rejuvenating and immunising. Together they number over 60 formulations. Immunity against disease and longevity are the goals of *rasayana*. The process of ageing is slowed down through this therapy.

There are three kinds of promotive treatments. One kind — *ajasrika* — is carried out in the form of a nutritious diet on a continuous basis. This involves the regular consumption of milk, clarified butter (*ghee*) and other such items of diet by way of direct nourishment. Food consumed every day should comprise these nourishing substances.

Kamya rasayana is administered in order to promote vigour and vitality. It does this in three ways:
* By promoting both vitality and longevity—*prana-kamya*
* By promoting the intellect in terms of intelligence and memory—*medha-kamya*
* By promoting a healthy complexion, giving it a glow and lustre—*sri-kamya*
    The third kind of promotive treatment is administered to promote vitality

While undertaking the indoor promotive treatment, it is essential to ensure that the residence is built on auspicious ground, facing the east or north.

of a specific kind. Known as *naimittika rasayana*, it is used for patients with specific diseases. Since promotive treatment is meant as preparatory to aphrodisiac therapies, the individual must be made fit enough to receive them. Even if aphrodisiac therapy is not undertaken, promotive treatment by itself can tone up the system and rejuvenate the individual. Each tissue element in the body is nourished through this.

Two methods are offered for promotive treatment: indoor treatment or *kutipravesika*; and treatment in the open air or *vatatapika*. The second method permits the individual to go about his normal duties and allows him to be exposed to normal air and sun conditions. This therapy is inexpensive and convenient and does not involve any special measures or precautions. It is, however, less effective in its impact.

Indoor treatment or *kutipravesika* is done under controlled conditions. There is an interesting description of the location for this therapy described in the *Charaka Samhita*: A cottage should be built on auspicious ground (which fulfils the requirements as given in the *Sastras*), facing eastward or northward and located in an area inhabited by the king, physicians and Brahmans (priests). It should be free from dangers. It should be sufficiently spacious in terms of area and height of the structure, with three concentric chambers one after the other with a small opening. The walls should be thick and impervious to sound, particularly to undesirable noises in the vicinity. The chambers should also be comfortable in all seasons, clean and favourable for habitation. Women should

41

The outdoors, fresh air and sunlight go a long way in promoting good health.

not be allowed near it (since such treatment is generally meant for men). It should be well equipped with all the necessities and be attended by physicians with medicaments as well as Brahmans.

The attitude towards *rasayana* is prayerful. As is customary on all auspicious occasions, the gods are invoked and the blessings of the Brahmans are sought by offerings made to both. An auspicious day and hour are selected for commencing the *rasayana* therapy.

The *rasayana* therapy begins with an unctuous massage and evacuation of the bowels. *Haritaki* (*Chebulic myrobala*), rock salt, *amalaka* (*Embelic myrobalan* or gooseberry), *vaca* (sweet flag), *vidanga* (*Embelia ribes*), jaggery, *haridra* (turmeric), *pippali* (long pepper) and dry ginger should be powdered and taken with hot water. After that a barley preparation with clarified butter (*ghee*) is given for three, five or seven days (according to the desired measure of evacuation until the bowels are cleansed). The appropriate drug is then administered by the physician with due consideration for the patient's age, constitution and suitability.

There are several recipes with *amalaki* and *haritaki* in *rasayana* therapies in Agnivesa's classical work as redacted by Charaka. An entire chapter has been

devoted to *rasayana* that includes several other drugs and fruits.
Other important *rasayanas* are:

❖ *Samisa mahamasa taila rasayana* (vegetarian and non-vegetarian)
❖ *Karikuranga rasayana* (therapy with meat and black gram oil)
❖ *Kapikacchu rasayana* (with meat of a black monkey)
❖ *Vasanta kusuma rasayana* (with substances translated as a friend of the god of love, Kama deva; this is both a *rasayana* and an aphrodisiac)

Vajikarana: Aphrodisiac Therapy

Vajikarana or aphrodisiac therapy, if taken on a regular basis, is believed to be extremely helpful in promoting longevity, virility, potency, great personal charm, mental and intellectual agility and the capacity to produce healthy offspring who will be a source of pride to the family and carry on its lineage for several generations.

According to the *Astanga-hrdaya* of Vagabhata:
Man who is seeking pleasure should resort to *vajikarana* (virilification) therapy constantly. It bestows contentment, nourishment, children with good qualities, continuity of progeny and great happiness immediately.

Astanga-hrdaya: Uttarasthana: 40:1

Charaka in his *Charaka Samhita* says:
Love, strength, happiness, professional excellency, widespread influence, vastness of kinsmen, fame, utility to the world, *sukhodarka* (that which gives happiness at a later stage), pleasure – all these are dependent upon children. Therefore a person desirous of children and the qualities associated with them should use

~

Charaka maintained that a woman, above all, was the greatest aphrodisiac.

~

aphrodisiacs daily if he wants satisfaction of worldly desires (*kama*) and happiness (*sukha*).

The *Sushruta Samhita* enumerates some of the things that can act as stimulants:

Various kinds of (nutritious and palatable) food and (sweet, luscious and refreshing) liquid cordials, speech that gladdens the ears, and touch which seems delicious to the skin, clear lights mellowed by the beams of the full moon and damsels young, beautiful and gay, dulcet songs that charm the soul and captivate the mind, use of betel leaves, wine and wreaths of (sweet-scented) flowers and a merry careless heart—these are the best aphrodisiacs in life.

Charaka, however, has the last word on the subject of aphrodisiacs:

All the objects of beauty are assembled in a woman in a compact form, and nowhere else. All the objects of the senses found in the person of a woman evoke the maximum delight in a man. The woman is, therefore, the most lovable object for a man. It is the woman who procreates children. *Dharma* (righteousness), *artha* (wealth), *lakshmi* (auspiciousness) and the entire world (*loka*) are established in a woman. The woman who is beautiful and youthful, who is endowed with auspicious signs, and who is amiable and skilled is the aphrodisiac *par excellence*.

Such a woman is also well versed in the sixty-four arts (*kalas*) such as vocal and instrumental music and dance as described in the *Kama Sastra* and is endowed with all the desirable qualities that would render her attractive. The *Kama Sutra* waxes eloquent about the woman who displays her creativity and skill in painting and making *mandala* (*tantrika*) designs on the floor where the family deities are worshipped; who can make delectable dishes in her neat and well-appointed kitchen; who is also skilled in preparing aphrodisiac recipes and herbal charms; who can thread together sweet-smelling flowers into wreaths; blend perfumes; and is well-versed in sewing and embroidery. Such a woman would also know the art of love and how to keep her husband happy. And this happiness would be reflected in his healthy and robust physique and the lustre

~

Charaka stated that righteousness, wealth, auspiciousness and the entire world were established in a woman.

~

acquired by his complexion. His interest in everything around him would also be aroused. Ideally speaking, a woman whose very presence delights her partner and arouses him sexually is the ultimate aphrodisiac – the *erotica ultimata*.

Aphrodisiacs play a large part in promoting the sexual urge. At any given time the sexual act can give satisfaction and be fulfilling only when there is the desire for sex in both partners and when both are mentally and physically fit. Anger, hatred, violent feelings, disinterest and other such negative factors have the opposite effect. Aphrodisiacs, therefore, are as necessary as tonics which are taken to supplement food intake. The upkeep of the human body, mind and intellect can be satisfactorily achieved by the constant use of aphrodisiacs.

The kinds of aphrodisiacs that can be useful, the frequency of their use, the age of the individual, the physical strength and the *prakruti* (constitution) are factors that determine *vajikarana* therapy with the goal of not only promoting sexual capacity and performance, but also greatly improving the physical and psychological health of an individual. Such a therapy is of great importance to young couples starting their lives together as well as to those who wish to continue their lives as productive members of society.

In the ancient past, aphrodisiacs were taken as a matter of routine before sexual intercourse. While Manu laid stress on the bringing forth of progeny, Vatsyayana emphasised the pleasurable aspect of sex. The physician's role must be to

~

Aphrodisiacs improve physical and psychological health, contributing to the overall upkeep of the body, mind and intellect.

~

maintain a balance between the two: the pleasure derived from the act can help motivate procreation. On the one hand impotence is an ailment while excess sexual activity can cause loss of tissue strength or *dhatus* and lead to diseases such as consumption. Likewise many children can also be a bane to parents, whereas infertility can also cause problems in a family.

Substances used for aphrodisiac therapy (*vajikarana dravyas*) are classified into three groups:

❖ Those which promote physical strength and semen—*deha-balakara* or *janaka*
❖ Those which enhance mental power (sexual potency)—*mano-balakara* or *pravartaka*
❖ Those which promote physical stength and semen and enhance mental power—*deha-mano-balakara* or *janaka pravartaka*

Examples of these substances are cowlage (*Mucuna prurita*), black gram (*Phaseolus radiatus*), Indian kudju (*Ipomoea digitata*), asparagus (*Asparagus racemosus*), winter cherry (*Withania somnifera*), liquorica (*Glycrrhiza glabra*), eggs, semen of animals and birds, testicles of goats and others. Cannabis was not used as an aphrodisiac in earlier times.

Rejuvenation and aphrodisiac therapies are grouped in terms of semen:

❖ For increasing semen—*sukravrddhikara*
❖ For promoting discharge or ejaculation—*sukrasrutikara*
❖ For increasing semen and promoting discharge or ejaculation—*sukrasruti vrddikara*

Recommended drugs

Various drugs, either single or in compound formulations, are advocated in all classical Ayurvedic texts as part of sexo-pharmacology. Examples of some are as follows:

Single drugs: Conitech cowlage, asparagus, black gram, liquorice, dried ginger, winter cherry, land cattrops, marking nut, white musali, nutmeg and pellitory for instance.

Compound formulations: *Vrsyagutika* (aphrodisiacal virility pills), *Vrsya-ghrta* (aphrodisiacal medicated clarified butter), *Vajikarana ghrta* (aphrodisiacal medicated clarified butter), *Mamsa-rasa* (meat soup), *Vrsya mamsarasa* (virile meat soup), *Apatyakara ghrta* (medicated clarified butter which helps in conception), *Vanari gulika* (pills made with cowlage), *Amrta bhallataka lehya*

Being loving, strong, free from anger, sexually inclined and capable of being excited helps in aphrodisiac therapies.

(rejuvenating recipe in linctus form made from marking nut), *Kamesvara modaka* (sweet confection for use as sexual stimulant), and many others.

Recommended dietary substances

Black gram (*masa*), wheat (*godhuma*), clarified butter (*ghrta*), milk (*ksira*), honey (*madhu*), sugar (*sarkara*), a variety of rice (*sali*), sugarcane (*iksu*), meat soup (*mamsa rasa*), buffalo meat soup (*mahisa rasa*).

Psycho-sexo-pharmacology

The psychological factors that help in aphrodisiac therapies are: being loving, strong, free from anger, sexually inclined and capable of being excited.

Most single drugs or compound formulations used in *vajikarana* or aphrodisiac therapy, including dietary elements, have a profound impact on the semen, the ovum and the genital organs of both males and females.

Drugs recommended for men:

- *Sukrajanaka*—procreator of semen
- *Sukravardhaka*—promoter of semen in quantity and quality
- *Sukrastambhaka*—prevention of premature ejaculation
- *Sukra-sravaka*—helps secrete semen
- *Vrsya*—promotes virility in both men and women
- *Sukra sodhaka*—purifier of semen

Drugs recommended for women:

- *Artava* or *rajas*-increases the production of ova
- *Artava janaka*—induces menstruation/ovulation
- *Artava sodhaka*—purifies the ovum
- *Artava rodhaka*—inhibits excessive flow of menstruation
- *Yoni sodhaka*—cleanses the vagina
- *Yoni daurgandhyanasaka*—destroys foul smell
- *Yoni sravakaraka*—lubricates the vagina
- *Yoni srava stambhaka*—prevents excessive secretion from the vagina
- *Yoni dardhyakaraka*—strengthens the loose vaginal muscles

Aphrodisiac Recipes

*a*ncient texts such as the *Charaka Samhita, Sushruta Samhita* and others are replete with recipes involving the use of drugs and dietary substances used in aphrodisiac therapy or *vajikarana.* The recipes however need to be modified to suit various kinds of constitutions, while taking into account the age, physical strength and other factors. Basically speaking, diet and regimen are directed towards the maintenance of a balanced constitution according to one's age, inherited physical and mental condition and the environment around.

Aphrodisiac therapies focus on the promotion of semen (*sukra*) both in terms of quantity and quality. In this lies the health of future generations—the goal being to procreate healthy progeny.

Sukra (semen) and *ojas* (the vital essence—*élan vitae*) are two important elements that need to be fostered. *Ojas* is that which:

> Maintains all living beings by its saturation; and without which no life of creatures exists; which is the initial essence of the embryo and also the essence of its nourishing material, which enters into the cardiac cycle first, which destroyed leads to destruction, which is the sustainer and located in the heart, which is the cream of the nutrient fluid in the body, and where vital factors are established, is the fruit of them or they produce various types of fruits (effects). Hence they (vessels) are called a *mahaphala* (which are important or have a great variety of benefits.)
>
> *Charaka: Sutra 30: 1-11*

~

Ojas is the essence of life, imparting virility and vigour, the cream of the nutrient fluid in the body. It provides virility, health and vigour.

~

Thus *ojas* is found in the heart; eight drops of *ojas* in an individual's body signifies an excellent type and is known as *para ojas*. *Ojas* being the essence of life, its presence is always felt. It imparts potency, virility, health, vigour and dynamism. The decrease of *ojas* is manifested in lack of virility, impotence, lassitude and listlessness. Its total absence signifies the end of life. *Ojas* and *sukra* therefore need to be promoted and care should be taken to see that the reserves of these two elements do not get depleted.

There are several articles of diet which, if taken in moderate quantities and along with nutritious food, can be stimulating and appetising despite the fact

The ojas *or nutritious element in the body is cooling and imparts dynamism. Alcohol, on the other hand, is heat giving and a depressant.*

that these substances may not have much intrinsic value as food. Wine and spirits, for instance, have properties which are directly opposite to *ojas*.

The ten properties of *ojas* are that it is heavy, cooling, soft, smooth, viscous, sweet, stable, clear, slimy and unctuous. Alcohol, on the other hand, is light, heat giving, enters the system easily, is sour and sharp in taste, gets quickly absorbed and acts swiftly. It is rough, acts as a depressant and is non-slimy. Normally speaking, alcohol and wine counteract the good effects of the *ojas* in an individual. Wine and alcohol must be imbibed in *sattvic* (pleasant) company. The *sattvika* party comprises companions who are polite and courteous in their speech, well versed in the arts, friendly and happy. Drinking with them is a pleasurable experience. The *rajasa* drinking party is full of people who possess a wrathful disposition, are emotional and melodramatic in their movements, angry and rude. They are boorish and unkempt in their appearance and habits. The *tamasa* party is that which is full of people who are generally dissatisfied and harbour excessive anger; they are in a state of stupor and sleep.

Ojas is severely affected if wine and spirits are taken immoderately and in excess. It is severely damaged in such cases particularly towards the last stages of drinking. Such deterioration in the *ojas* can lead to consumption and acute dermatitis, and at times, even death.

Wine, however, if taken in proper quantities, intoxicates mildly and produces exhilaration, energy, contentment, sexual potency, strength and freedom from disorders. It endows one with a good physique. To obtain the maximum benefit from wine, it is necessary to drink in good company and in moderate quantities. Nourishing food should be taken alongside.

> 🦢 Wine made of many ingredients and possessed of many properties and actions and characterised by intoxication has both merits and demerits. It is like nectar for he who drinks according to prescribed methods, in proper quantity, at the proper time, with wholesome food, according to one's strength and with exhilaration. On the contrary, it acts like poison for him who indulges in drinking unwholesome wine whenever it is presented, observing rough regimens and physical exertion constantly.
>
> *Charaka: Chikitsa* 24: 26-28

Milk also has attributes similar to *ojas* and semen (*sukra*). Milk is given an important place in one's dietary regimen in Ayurveda. It is an essential element in aphrodisiac therapy. Milk and clarified butter (*ghee*) have nourishing qualities and the positive attributes of milk are manifold. Milk is recommended before sexual intercourse as well as afterwards. It is said to promote the production of semen. The absence of milk in one's diet can lead to problems. In today's world of pasteurised milk and additives, it is not uncommon to find many people with lactose intolerance.

Cow's milk, given with honey, sugar and clarified butter is an excellent aphrodisiac.

~

Charaka's recommendation of milk as part of aphrodisiac therapy emphasises the excellent qualities of cow's milk:

One should keep the milch cow fed on black gram leaves or sugarcane or *arjuna* leaves, well-nourished, with four nipples, of brown or black colour and having one live calf of the same colour, with her horns pointing upwards and giving thick milk. The milk of such a cow alone, either boiled or unboiled, with sugar added along with honey and *ghee* (clarified butter) is an excellent aphrodisiac.

Charaka: Chikitsa 2:3: 3-5

One who desires inexhaustible semen should use milk boiled with semen-promoting, life-promoting, corpulence-promoting, strength-promoting and galactagogue groups of drugs separately, and add to it wheat flour along with *ghee* (clarified butter), honey and sugar.

Charaka: Chikitsa 2:3:6-7

The milk of the aforesaid cow (see above) boiled with a golden ring and with *ghee* (clarified butter), honey and sugar added afterwards provides progeny.

Charaka: Chikitsa 2:3:11

Any substance which is sweet, unctuous, makes the body stout, increases strength and is pleasing to the mind—each of them is called *vrsya* (aphrodisiac).

Astanga-hrdya: Uttara 40:35

Thus Charaka in the *chikitsa* (treatment) section in his work *Charaka Samhita* has offered an aphrodisiac recipe:

🪳 *Ghee* (clarified butter), *masa* (black gram) and the testicles of a he-goat should be boiled with the soup of buffalo's meat. This should be fried in freshly made *ghee* after adding sour fruits to it. To this recipe add a little salt, coriander, cumin and ginger. This is an excellent recipe for the promotion of virility, strength and nourishment.

Charaka: Chikitsa 2:2:42-43

Milk should be boiled by adding the powder of asparagus. Intake of this milk, to which sugar is added, produces an aphrodisiac effect in as much as the genital organ continues to remain hard and erect even after sexual intercourse.

The juice of the root of a well-grown silk-cotton tree should be mixed with sugar. Intake of this juice continuously for seven days enhances the quantity of semen profusely.

The roots of a tender silk-cotton tree (*salmali*) and black musli (*tala-musli*) should be made into a powder. Intake of this powder with clarified butter (*ghee*) and milk enables a person to enjoy sex frequently.

The powder of the tuberous root of Indian kudju (*vidari/ipomea*) should be taken along with clarified butter (*ghee*), milk and fig juice. This rejuvenates even an old person to be as sexually active as a youth.

The powder of gooseberry (emblic myrobalan) should be impregnated with its own juice. Intake of this impregnated powder with clarified butter and honey works as an aphrodisiac.

A goat's testicle should be fried with clarified butter made out of milk (not yoghurt). Intake of this along with the powder of long pepper and salt promotes virility.

Milk boiled along with a goat's testicles, and flavoured with sesame seeds, makes an excellent aphrodisiac.

The powder of Indian kudju should be mixed with its own juice. Taken with clarified butter and honey, this works as an aphrodisiac.

If the powders of conitech cowlage seeds and long-leaved barleria are mixed with sugar and eaten with freshly collected cow's milk, the aphrodisiac effect is potent.

〜

Following pages 56-67: Aphrodisiacs play an important part in promoting the sexual urge. They act as tonics and food supplements.

〜

Intake of the powder of the root of *uccata* (white chaff flower) either alone or with the powder of asparagus, in combination with milk, has an aphrodisiac effect.

Ten grams of the powder of liquorice (*glycyrrhiza*) should be mixed with clarified butter and honey. Taking this with milk promotes virility.

The powder of land cattrops (*goksura*), long-leaved barleria, roots of asparagus, conitech cowlage, country mallow and *atibala* (a variety of country mallow) should be taken at night with milk to promote virility.

The powder of the seeds of black gram should be fried with clarified butter and then boiled by adding milk. Intake of this milk preparation is an excellent aphrodisiac.

Intake of milk boiled by adding the root, fruit, bark and aerial root of the sacred fig tree promotes virility.

Milk boiled along with the seeds of conitech cowlage, seeds of land cattrops, the root of white chaff flower and sugar makes for an excellent aphrodisiac.

A mixture of sugar, dehusked black gram, bamboo-salt, milk, clarified butter and wheat flour should be made into a paste. Dividing it into equal portions, pancakes should be made by frying with clarified butter. When soft, these pancakes should be added to a hot and

The therapeutic effects of rasayana *and* vajikarana *benefit those who pursue righteousness as a way of life.*

aromatic chicken soup and then removed in a semi-solid form. These pancakes have excellent aphrodisiac qualities. As a substitute for chicken soup, the soup of the meat of a peacock, partridge or duck may also be used.

Another way of promoting virility is by eating sparrow meat and then following it up with milk.

Several aphrodisiac recipes containing plants, metals and minerals are described in Ayurvedic texts. Some of the commonly and popularly used recipes are:

❧ *Narasimha-curna* (powdered form of land cattrops): This is prepared in the form of a powder. The main ingredients are asparagus, land cattrops, *guduci*, marking nut and sesame seeds.

❧ *Godhumadya-ghrta* (medicated clarified butter made with wheat): This is a recipe of medicated clarified butter. The main ingredients are wheat, winter cherry, marking nut, conitech cowlage and clarified butter.

❧ *Brhat-asvagandha-ghrta* (medicated clarified butter): This is also a recipe for medicated clarified butter. The main ingredients are winter cherry, clarified butter, milk and conitech cowlage.

❧ *Brhat-satavari-ghrta* (medicated clarified butter with asparagus): Yet another recipe of medicated clarified butter, the main ingredients are asparagus root, milk, clarified butter and honey.

❧ *Kamadeva-ghrta* (medicated clarified butter with a substance named after the god of love): This medicated clarified butter is made with winter cherry, asparagus, Indian kudju, part of the sacred fig tree, lotus seeds, conitech cowlage, kuth and black gram.

❧ *Brhat-satavari-medaka* (bollus made with asparagus): This is an aphrodisiac prepared in the form of a sweetmeat. The main ingredients are asparagus, land cattrops, country mallow, common mallow, conitech cowlage, long-leaved baleria, buffalo milk, purified cannabis, musk and camphor.

❧ *Rativallabha-modaka* (a sexually stimulating bollus): Also prepared in the form of a sweetmeat, the main ingredients are seeds of cannabis, clarified butter, sugar, asparagus, cow's milk, goat's milk, musk, camphor and honey.

Kamesvara-modaka (a sexually stimulating confection): The ingredients of this preparation are calcined powder of mica, purified sulphur, detoxicated cannabis, fenugreek, resin of the silk-cotton tree, Indian kudju, black musali, land cattrops, long-leaved baleria, kuth, asparagus, liquorice, nutmeg and contitech cowlage. They are prepared as a sweetmeat.

Madanananda-modaka (a sweetmeat made with purified mercury): Prepared as a sweetmeat, the main ingredients are purified mercury, purified sulphur, calcined powder of mica, camphor, long pepper, *kuotha* or a decoction, nutmeg, Indian kudju, asparagus, liquorice, country mallow, common mallow, conitech cowlage, land cattrops, cannabis, milk and sugar.

Vanari-vatika (cowlage pills): Taken in the form of pills, the main ingredients are conitech cowlage, milk and sugar.

Amrtaprasa-ghrta (rejuvenating clarified butter): This is a type of medicated clarified butter prepared in the form of a linctus. The main ingredients are clarified butter made of cow's milk, goat's meat, winter cherry, country mallow, land cattrops, conitech cowlage, musk and sugar.

Sri-Gopala-taila (externally applied oil): A medicated oil, the main ingredients are sesame oil, asparagus, embellic myrobalan, country mallow, winter cherry, land cattrops, costus, testicles of a civet cat, saffron, musk and amber. This medicated oil is taken internally and also applied over the genital organs of males and females as well as the breasts of women to promote virility.

Mrga-mada taila (medicated oil with musk): This is a medicated oil prepared with sesame oil, musk, pellitory and the oil of bitter almonds. If used externally, it causes erection and sturdiness of the male organ.

Svalpa-candrodaya-makaradhvaja (pills with mercury, sulphur, gold): This is a pill prepared with nutmeg, cloves, camphor, black pepper, musk and a preparation of purified mercury and purified sulphur. It is a powerful aphrodisiac, and promoter of strength, digestive power and semen.

❧ *Purna-Candrodaya-rasa* (pills with mercury, sulphur, gold, musk): This is prepared in a pill form. First of all, a purified gold leaf is triturated with purified mercury. This forms an amalgam. Purified sulphur is added to this and triturated till the entire mixture is reduced to a fine black powder form. In Ayurvedic parlance this is called *kajjali*. This black powder is then added to the juice of the red flower of the cotton tree and Aloe Indica, and dried. Thereafter the mixture ought to be put into a glass bottle which is wrapped with seven layers of dried mud-smeared cloth and cooked in a *baluka-yantra* (vessel with sand). To begin with, it should be cooked on a mild fire. The neck of the bottle should be kept clean with the help of an iron rod. When the sulphur fumes stop coming out and the bottom of the bottle looks red, the opening of the bottle must be closed with a cork made out of calcium stone and then sealed with a paste containing jaggery and lime. Thereafter, strong heat should be employed by which the mixture at the bottom will get sublimed and adhere to the neck of the bottle. After it has cooled down the bottle should be broken and the sublimed material scraped out of the neck. This process is called *makaradhvaja*.

The gold left at the bottom of the bottle is then added to the scraped-out material and triturated by adding ingredients like camphor, nutmeg, musk and black pepper. Pills of 250 mg are made out of this paste. This is an excellent aphrodisiac recipe to rejuvenate the body. It is best taken with betel leaf and the person taking it should drink a good quantity of milk and eat heavy food to enjoy its best effects.

There are several other recipes in this type such as *Makaradhvaja-rasa* (mixture of gold, mercury, sulphur and other substances), *Svarna–sindura* (mixture of gold, mercury, sulphur).

❧ *Kamini-darpaghna-rasa* (pills with purified mercury and sulphur): This is prepared in a pill form. Purified mercury and purified sulphur are triturated together; this forms a black powder called *kajjali*. The purified seeds of stramonium are added to this; the mixture is triturated again by adding the oil extracted from stramonium seeds. This is a strong aphrodisiac.

❧ *Purnacandra-rasa* (pills with purified mercury and sulphur for sexual stimulation): This is prepared in the form of pills. It contains a preparation of purified mercury and purified sulphur, mineral pitch, *Emblica ribes* and purified copper pyrites which are triturated with honey and clarified butter.

❧ *Dasmularista* (medicated wine): A medicated wine prepared with several herbs and musk, it promotes virility.

❧ *Vasanta-kusumakara* (pills made with calcined powders): Prepared in the form of pills, this contains calcined powders of gold, silver, tin, lead, iron, mica, corals and pearls. The powder is impregnated and triturated with milk and the juice of the decoction made of eight other herbs, added with musk and saffron. This is then made into pills. These pills are taken along with big pieces of crystal sugar (*misri*), honey and clarified butter. A popular aphrodisiac, this is also a cure for diabetes mellitus.

The ingredients of a few aphrodisiac recipes are given here as illustrations of the kind of substances used in aphrodisiac therapy. There is a virtual storehouse of such recipes in ancient Ayurvedic texts waiting to be unearthed.

❧ *Asvagandhadi Lehya* (Winter cherry-*Withania somnifera*): A linctus
(Source: *Pharmacopoeia of Hospital of Integrated Medicine,* Chennai, India)

Sugar (*sarkara*)	1.356 kg
Winter cherry (*asvagandha curna*-powder)	192 gm
Hemi desmus indicus (*sariva curna*-root)	192 gm
Powdered cumin (*jiraka curna*-fruit)	192 gm
Colchicum powder (*madhusnuhi curna*-rhizome)	192 gm
Grapes (*draksa*-dry fruit)	192 gm
Clarified butter (*ghrta*)	226 gm
Honey	452 gm
Cardamom powder (*ela curna*-seed)	24 gm
Water	452 ml

✳ *Dosage:* 6 to 12 gm

Substance (*anupana*) to be taken with milk

Important therapeutic use: balya (strength promoting), *rasayana* (promotive treatement), *vajikarana* (rejuvenation therapy)

※ *Makaradhvaja* (see p. 61)

(Source: *Bhaisajyaratnavali Vajikaranadhikara: 237-238*)

Gold (*svarna*)	12 gm
Mercury (*parada*)	96 gm
Sulphur (*gandhaka*)	288 gm
Juice of the flower of the red silk-cotton tree (*rakta karpasa kusuma*)	Q.S. (for trituration)
Juice of aloe vera (*kumari*)	Q.S (for trituration)

Special method of preparation: Purified mercury is put into a *khalva* (pestle and mortar) and purified *svarna patra* (gold leaf) is dissolved by trituration. Then purified *gandhaka curna* (sulphur powder) is added in small quantities and carefully ground to form a *kajjali* (black powder). Later the *svarasas* or juices are added one by one and ground. The mixture is dried and put in a *kacakupi* (glass bottle) and prepared by the usual method in the *valuka yantra* (sand-filled vessel).

✶ *Dosage:* 125 mg

Substance (*anupana*): With betel leaves, milk, honey

Important therapeutic use: Hrddaurbalya (cardiac weakness), *rasayana* (promotive treatment) and *vajikarana* (rejuvenation therapy).

Other aphrodisiac recipes may also be mentioned as examples. These include: *Satavari modaka* (asparagus-based bollus), *Sukramatrka vati* (pills for promoting semen production), *Sukrastambhaka vati* (pills for delaying ejaculation) and *Navaratnarajamrganka rasa* (pills made with precious stones). The last one in this list contains 57 ingredients and has to be prepared in a very elaborate and time-consuming manner. The recipe can be found in *Yogaratnakara Rajayaksma Chikitsa: p.331.*

Apart from these elaborately prepared recipes containing herbs, minerals and substances from the animal kingdom, there are several food items used in most homes all over the world that have aphrodisiac properties. There are also others which are contraindicated if aphrodisiac therapy is being used.

Among seafood the following are recommended: lobsters, crabs, prawns and shrimps. Chicken, sparrow meat and eggs promote the production of semen. Mushrooms, artichokes and asparagus are also good for the same purpose. Spices

Ardhamatsyendra asana
(Half Spinal Twist posture)

Janu Sirsa asana
(Knee and Head
posture)

Simha asana
(Lion posture)

Pranayama
(Breath control)

and condiments such as cumin seeds, cardamoms, cloves, ginger, garlic and jaggery are also recommended. Nuts like almonds, cashew, pistachio are recommended. Curds, alcohol, tobacco, coriander seeds, cannabis and heroin have attributes opposite to milk and are regarded as inhibitors of semen and virility. As stated earlier, milk is highly recommended. It is said to have ten attributes similar to semen.

All the recipes and food items mentioned above are those which heighten sexual fulfilment and keep the body fit for sexual activity.

Another aspect of Indian thought that can help in problems relating to virility is yoga—a complete system in itself. *Hatha* yoga advocates the following *asanas* or body positions:

Paschimottana asana (Posterior Stretch posture), *Janusira asana* (Knee and Head posture), *Dhanur asana* (Bow pose), *Sirsa asana* (Headstand posture), *Ardha-matsyendrasana* (Half Spinal Twist posture), *Simha asana* (Lion posture), *Siddha asana* (Perfect posture), *Baddhapadma asana* (Lotus pose), *Mula bandha* (Yogic posture), *Uiddiyana bandha* (Yogic posture), *Nadi shodana* (Breathing exercise), *Antarika kumbhaka* (Retention of breath in breathing exercise), *Dhyana* (Meditation), *Pranayama* (Breath control).

If practised under the guidance of a good tutor, yoga can be of immense benefit to every individual.

Plants, Herbs and Substances Used as Aphrodisiacs

CONITECH COWLAGE ✦ *Atmagupta*
Mucuna pruriens

Description: A slender climbing annual, it has 15 to 22 cm-long leaves and flowers with purplish corollas. The pods are 5 to 7 cm long with bean-shape seeds which are white in colour.

Habitat: Conitech cowlage grows wild in the foothills of the Himalayas and in the plains all over India and Sri Lanka.

Use in the reproductive system: The plant has been successfully tried out in promoting male virility. It is, however, generally used in combination with other medicines.

General use: Found to be useful in the treatment of Parkinson's disease, it is also used to remove general weakness.

FENUGREEK ✦ *Methi*
Trigonella Foenum-graecum

Description: A small plant, fenugreek grows up to 1 to 2 feet in height when full grown. The leaves are trifoliate, roundish, half inch to 1-1/2 inches long. The flowers are white or yellow and blossom in ones and twos, along with new leaves. The seeds are found in the pods which are nearly six centimetres long and hairy.

Habitat: This herb is an annual and is found growing wild. It is found extensively in Kashmir, Punjab, Mumbai and Chennai and is also cultivated far and wide.

Use in the reproductive system: Fenugreek seeds act as an aphrodisiac and also as an emmenagogue (a substance which causes menstruation). In addition, they have a diuretic effect. Used in a recipe for gruel, the seeds are given to nursing mothers. Pessaries (vaginal suppositeries) made of fenugreek are used in cases of leucorrhoea.

General use: Tender shoots of the plant, the aromatic leaves and dried seeds are used widely in Indian cuisine. The seeds are mucilaginous, demulcent and diuretic. They also act as a tonic, carminative, astringent and emollient (soothing agent). They stimulate the appetite. Fried in clarified butter (*ghee*) and mixed with aniseed, they help stop diarrhoea.

SENSITIVE PLANT ♦ *Lajjalu*
Mimosa pudica

Description: The Sensitive Plant, as it is known, responds to touch and is a rapidly growing shrub found in many places. The stem and stalk are thorny and they have long brittle bristles. The leaves are compound and sensitive to touch. The leaflets are in pairs of 15 to 20. The roots branch out in all directions and are reddish-brown, cylindrical and tapering. The flowers are mauve to pink with a minute calyx. The pods are also covered with fine bristles. The roots, leaves and seeds are used in medicine.

Habitat: This shrub grows wild as a weed in India in the more humid and warm regions. It also grows in the tropical regions of Africa, America and Brazil.

Use in the reproductive system: The use of the Sensitive Plant as a medicine is mentioned by both Charaka and Sushruta. It is commonly used for bleeding disorders like menorrhagia. The root used in the form of a decoction is found to be useful in urinary complaints. It is also known to have aphrodisiac properties. The seeds help to increase the production of semen and provide vigour and vitality in the male. The sperm count also increases. This plant is also used in the treatment of leucorrhoea.

General use: The root and leaves are crushed and powdered and are used in the treatment of piles and fistula. The juice made from the leaves has antiseptic properties and helps to purify the blood.

NUX VOMICA ✦ *Visa-musti*
Strychnos nuxvomica

Description: A deciduous tree found throughout India, the leaves are shiny and elliptical and the tree has a thin grey bark. The flowers are greenish-white, while the fruits appear in the form of bitter red berries.

Habitat: It is found growing wild in the jungles on both the east and west coasts of Tamil Nadu, Kerala and Orissa.

Use in the reproductive system: Nux vomica seeds must be used carefully under medical supervision. Habitual use is known to be addictive. They have aphrodisiac properties and are found to be effective in cases of impotence.

General use: Purified nux vomica helps in eliminating constipation, loss of digestive power and similar disorders. It is also found useful in the treatment of asthma and epilepsy.

LAND CATTROPS/PUNCTURE VINE ✦ *Goksura*
Tribulus terrestris

Description: A perennial trailing plant, its fruits are globose and contain several seeds.

Habitat: Land cattrops grows wild all over India and in Africa up to altitudes of 3000 metres. It thrives in well-irrigated soil.

Use in the reproductive system: Land cattrops, along with other drugs in recipes, is an excellent aphrodisiac even for the elderly. It also checks haemorrhages, particularly urethral. The plant and dried spiny fruits made into an infusin are used in cases of spermatorrhoea, urinary discorders, diseases of the genito-urinary system such as dysuria, gonorrhoea, incontinence, uterine disorders after parturition and in impotence.

General use: The fruit of land cattrops, powdered and mixed with other ingredients like winter cherry and honey mixed with milk, is useful in the treatment of consumption. It alleviates coughs. The root powdered with several drugs such as *Kokilaksa eranda,* wild eggplant and night shade and processed with milk and sweet curd, helps break calculus (collection of stones in the kidneys or gall bladder). Land cattrops is an essential part of several recipes which help in hair growth and lumbago.

COUNTRY MALLOW ✦ *Bala*
Sida cordifolia

Description: The plant is 1 to 5 feet tall and has strong roots (hence the name *bala*). It is a small herb, branched and hairy. The leaves are 2.5 to 5 cm long, egg-shaped, oblong with petioles (stalks joining the leaves to the stems) 1.2 to 3.8 cm long. The flowers are small and yellow and the fruits are like capsules, 6 to 8 mm in diameter.

Habitat: This small herb grows throughout the plains of India where the climate is damp and humid.

Use in the reproductive system: Country mallow is considered to be one of the most useful drugs in Ayurvedic medicine. The seeds are used in the treatment of gonorrhoea. The juice of the whole plant is found useful in spermatorrhoea, while a preparation along with other drugs is known to cure diseases of the generative organs. The powdered root bark is used in a recipe for the treatment of frequent urination and leucorrhoea. The root helps to strengthen the vagina and aids in easy delivery. The seeds are combined with other ingredients and used as an aphrodisiac. They are also found to be useful for impotence, seminal and other debilities, such as for increasing sperm count.

General use: The plant has anticonvulsant and antipyretic properties. It is useful in the treatment of bronchospasm, cough and fever. Country mallow oil is used in cases of difficult labour. Milk boiled with a decoction of country mallow and taken twice a day helps alleviate pain during childbirth. It is also used to cure scrotal enlargement.

SANDALWOOD ✦ *Chandana*
Santalum album

Description: A small evergreen tree, sandalwood has drooping branches. The heartwood is yellowish-brown and is strongly scented. The leaves are elliptical, long and slender and the flowers brownish-red, without any odour.

Habitat: It grows wild and is cultivated widely in Mysore and Coorg, Coimbatore, Salem and southern parts of Tamil Nadu.

Use in the reproductive system: Sandalwood is a popular remedy for the treatment of urethral haemorrhage and pruritis. Apart from this, sandalwood is also used in the treatment of urinary infection. It is an important ingredient in several aphrodisiac recipes.

General use: Ground into a paste with water, the wood is applied to local inflammations, to the temples in fever and in skin diseases.

DRUMSTICK TREE ✦ *Sirisa*
Albizzia lebbeck

Description: A big tree, 50 to 60 feet high, it grows wild and is also planted on roadsides for shade. The leaves are compound, with 4 to 8 pairs on each stalk. The pods are approximately 6 inches long and about 1 inch broad. In each pod there are about 8-10 seeds which are brown, flat and round.

Habitat: This tree is found all over India.

Use in the reproductive system: As a post-operative measure, in cases of confounded foetus, water processed with drumstick (*sirisa*) and *arjuna* is taken. It promotes virility.

General use: The juice of the drumstick flowers along with other ingredients is found to be efficacious in ailments where *kapha* (phelgm) and *pitta* (bile) are predominant. Drumstick flowers are also used in recipes for all types of asthma. Drumstick used in several recipes with other ingredients, has been found to be effective as an antidote to certain poisons and heals insect bites, particularly those of a poisonous nature.

HIBISCUS ✦ *Japa kusume*
Hibiscus rosa-sinensis

Description: A flowering plant whose dark green leaves make an attractive contrast to its red flowers, some hybrid varieties have lighter coloured leaves and white, yellow or pink flowers. Its roots are cylindrical, sweet to taste and mucilaginous. The leaves are whole at the base and coarsely toothed at the apex. The flowers are generally red in colour with five petals and are about 3 inches in diameter.

Habitat: The hibiscus is grown in gardens all over India as an ornamental plant.

Use in the reproductive system: In Ayurvedic literature hibiscus flowers are known to have anti-fertility effects. As a household remedy the flowers are crushed and sugar is added to the juice for controlling excessive uterine bleeding. They are also used in the treatment of menorrhagia. Some preliminary trials have also been carried out on the use of hibiscus as a contraceptive. It is also used to cure impotence and to promote virility.

General use: A black hair dye is prepared from the petals of the flower.

MARKING NUT ✦ *Bhallataka*
Somecarpus anacardium

Description: This is a tree, 20 to 30 feet high. The leaves are about 3 to 8 inches long and 5 to 12 inches broad. They appear at the top of tender branches. The fruit is juicy and yellow in colour when it matures. The seeds appear at the top of the thalamus; when ripe, they are black in colour. When the outer shell of the seed is removed, a cashew-like pulp appears which is eaten. To prevent allergic reactions, they are used only after processing (*sodhana* or purification) These are rubbed with brick powder, washed with warm water and then boiled with milk for detoxification. Milk, clarified butter and coconut are used as antidotes of its toxicity.

Habitat: It grows wild in the forests of eastern India.

Use in the reproductive system: The marking nut is used as an aphrodisiac, to strengthen the male genital organ and in dysmenorrhoea.

General use: Effective in indigestion, chronic constipation, sciatica, epilepsy, chronic fever, enlargement of the spleen and liver, leucoderma, eczema, psoriasis and general weakness, it also gets rid of intestinal parasites.

MUSK ✦ *Kasturi*
Moschus moschiferus

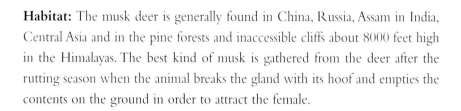

Description: Musk is a dried secretion from the preputial follicles of the male musk deer. It has a long-lasting, diffusible, strong odour and bitter aromatic taste.

Habitat: The musk deer is generally found in China, Russia, Assam in India, Central Asia and in the pine forests and inaccessible cliffs about 8000 feet high in the Himalayas. The best kind of musk is gathered from the deer after the rutting season when the animal breaks the gland with its hoof and empties the contents on the ground in order to attract the female.

Use in the reproductive system: Musk is a stimulant and aphrodisiac.

General use: It is a pain-reliever, anti-spasmodic, expectorant, laxative. It is used in perfumes and soaps and in children's nervous problems.

INDIAN KUDJU ✦ *Vidari*
Ipomoea digitata

Description: A large deciduous climber with a woody tuberculated stem, the Indian kudju is a perennial whose stems are long, thick, twining and tough. The leaves are broad, palmate and deeply divided. The flowers are pink and the seeds are covered with brownish hair.

Habitat: Found on the hills of the Konkan, the Deccan, in Karnataka, Orissa, Bihar, the Himalayas and Nepal, the warmer and moister the region, the more abundant is the growth.

Use in the reproductive system: It is used in diminished lactation, general debility and as a promoter of semen. It is also an aphrodisiac.

General use: Given as a demulcent and refrigerant in fevers, Indian kudju is used at times as an anetic and a tonic. It is also used to treat a sore throat.

SAFFRON ✦ *Kesara*
Crocus sativus

Description: The plant has a bulb and is onion like, approximately 1 to 1/2 feet high. Once grown, the plant yields flowers for 10 to 15 years. The stamens are three-eared with brilliant orange-red stigmas which are dried and used.

Habitat: Saffron was imported into India from Asia Minor and is now grown mainly in Kashmir. Spanish saffron is known to be of a very high quality. It is also cultivated in France, Italy and Turkey.

Use in the reproductive system: Saffron is known to have aphrodisiac properties and is safe to use in small quantities. It is useful in cases of general debility.

General use: It is successfully used in treating coughs and colds and decreased appetite.

INDIAN ALOE ✦ *Kumari*
Aloe indica

Description: The aloe has large, stemless, thick, fleshy leaves, lance like in shape with a sharp tip and spiny sides. Colours vary from species to species, but are generally green, grey and brown.

Habitat: Native to eastern and southern Africa, several species are found growing naturally in India in all regions. It is also cultivated throughout India.

Use in the reproductive system: Used as an emmenogogue and promotor of virility, the fresh juice of the leaves is used on the uterus and also in dysuria. The juice, made into a paste with cumin, helps in penile inflammation and in abcesses.

General use: The leaves are used in the treatment of ulcers, while the root is used in cases of colic. The fresh juice, along with other ingredients, helps in the alleviation of the enlargement of the spleen, scrofula (a disease with glandular swellings), epilepsy and palpitation.

Putrajivaka
Putranjiva roxburghii

Description: An evergreen tree, it is 9 to 12 m high with pendant branches and a pale and corky bark. The shining dark green leaves are 6 to 10 cm x 2.2 to 3.8 cm and are elliptical in shape. Male and female flowers are crowded in rounded clusters.

Habitat: This plant is found throughout tropical India, Sri Lanka and Myanmar. It grows naturally and is also cultivated.

Use in the reproductive system: The plant is fragrant, cooling and pungent and is an aphrodisiac.

General use: It is used as a laxative and diuretic. It is useful in billiousness, thirst, burning sensations and elephantiasis. The leaves, fruit and stones of the fruit are given in decoction form for colds and fevers.

ASAFOETIDA ✦ *Hingu*
Ferula narthex

Description: Asafoetida is an aromatic gum resin obtained by incision from the roots of a small plant; it has several varieties.

Habitat: It grows wild in the Punjab and the valley of Kashmir in India, in Iran and in Afghanistan.

Use in the reproductive system: It is a diuretic and aphrodisiac and an emmenagogue. It has also been found useful in the treatment of cases of habitual abortion. Asafoetida is given in gradually increasing doses in the form of pills when pregnancy is suspected. Thereafter, it is reduced till confinement.

General use: It is extremely useful in case of flatulance, colic, torpidity of the liver and indigestion where it is combined with other ingredients.

SACRED LOTUS ✦ *Kamala/Pankaja*
Nelumbo nucifera

Description: An aquatic herb, the lotus has a stout yellowish-white or brownish rhizome. The plant has floating leaves and flowers. Generally reddish in colour, the flowers are also white. The white lotus is somewhat rare. It is a sacred flower, is used widely in India in religious ceremonies and is venerated in Hinduism, Jainism and Buddhism.

Habitat: The red variety is found in tanks and ponds throughout India.

Use in the reproductive system: Found particularly useful in bleeding disorders, it is commonly prescribed for conception and for proper foetal development. It has been found useful in intrauterine growth retardation and in menorrhagia. The seeds are used as an aphrodisiac.

General use: The fleshy rhizomes are used as a treatment in diarrhoea and dysentery. The lotus also relieves fatigue and general weakness.

WHITE MUSALI ✦ *Saveta musali*
Asparagus adscendens

Description: The musali is a long, thin and thorny plant which grows tall and erect. Its leaves grow in tufts on the stalks. The rhizomes which are 0.25 to 0.5 cm thick, are white in colour.

Habitat: The plant is native to Gujarat, Madhya Pradesh and Hardwar in Uttar Pradesh. It also grows in the Himalayas.

Use in the reproductive system: The tuberous root and rhizome of the plant are used in medicine. It is known to be useful as an aphrodisiac as well as for increasing sperm count. Other benefits include combating general weakness.

General use: The tubers are found to be useful in the treatment of piles, asthma, jaundice, diarrhoea and colic.

ASPARAGUS ✦ *Satavari*
Asparagus racemosus

Description: The asparagus is a climber which grows up to 1 to 2 metres in length. The leaves are small and uniform and resemble pine needles. Tiny white flowers appear in small spikes. The roots grow in clusters and are shaped like fingers.

Habitat: This climber grows in low jungles all over India. It is also an attractive plant cultivated in homes and gardens.

Use in the reproductive system: Musali has been used in Indian medicine for centuries and has been mentioned by Charaka and Vagabhata. Its main use is as a galactagogue to increase milk secretion during lactation. It is also known to be useful for increasing the production of semen.

General use: Useful in cases of general debility, asparagus is an antispasmodic and a demulcent (soothing agent).

BLACK MUSLI ✦ *Talamuli*
Curculigo orchioides

Description: A small perennial, black musli has an elongated tuberous root, stalk and lateral roots. The plant has short petiolate leaves occurring in rosettes with bright yellow flowers.

Habitat: Black musali grows wild throughout the subtropical Himalaya from Kumaon eastwards, in Bengal and Assam. It is also found in western and southern India.

Use in the reproductive system: The root stalk and rhizome are used in both Ayurvedic and Unani remedies. Legends of ancient times state that it is a herb that endows an individual with a great deal of strength and also has effective aphrodisiac qualities. It is indicated in erectile impotence, spermatorrhoea and menorrhagia.

General use: This is used extensively in Ayurvedic formulations for a wide range of ailments, especially as a general tonic for weakness, fatigue and the treatment of piles. Tribals are known to use the rhizome powder in cooking as an edible flour.

CAMPHOR ✦ *Karpura*
Cinnamomum camphora

Description: Camphor is a concrete volatile oil obtained by distillation with water of the wood of the tree. It is purified by sublimation. Camphor is found in translucent white crystals.

Habitat: Camphor is available easily in Indian bazaars. The tree also grows in Borneo, Sumatra, Myanmar and in parts of India.

Use in the reproductive system: Pills of camphor and opium in certain proportions are found to be efficacious in cases of spermatorrhoea and pruritus. Camphor is also used in uterine pains and as a liniment. Camphor ointment is a very useful application in pruritus and eczema of the genitals and dysmenorrhoea. Several aphrodisiac recipes also use camphor.

General use: Camphor is used in a number of ailments such as epilepsy, acute rheumatism, toothache, chronic bronchitis, cold in the head.

MINERAL PITCH ✦ *Silajatu*

Description: This is an exudate from stones found in mountains. The pitch comes out of stones in the summer season because of exposure to the rays of the hot sun during the day. Depending upon the mineral content of the stone, mineral pitch is of four types: gold, silver, copper and iron. The last variety is commonly available and popularly used as an aphrodisiac and for rejuvenation of the body. It makes the body compact and strong like a stone. The stones having this pitch are generally inaccessible to human beings. Monkeys, birds, rats and other animals inhabiting these mountains generally eat away this natural mineral pitch. Since rats instinctively void stool in one place, the local people dissolve this excreta in water, process it and supply it as mineral pitch. For medical purposes, stones containing mineral pitch are boiled with water. The cream which comes out is used as mineral pitch in recipes. In its natural state it smells like cow's urine.

Habitat: The stones containing mineral pitch are available in the mountains of northern India (the Himalayas), Bhutan, Pakistan, Tibet, the Arab countries and Mongolia.

Use in the reproductive system: A strong aphrodisiac, it is popularly used for promotion of physical strength and rejuvenation of the body.

General use: Charaka has summarised the effect of mineral pitch as:
> There is no curable disease in this world which is not effectively cured by *silajatu* when administered at appropriate times in combination with useful drugs and by adopting the prescribed method.

By implication, this drug promotes general and specific immunity against diseases. Apart from the diseases of the genito-urinary system in both males and females, it is an excellent cure for diseases of the bones and joints.

SILK-COTTON TREE ✦ *Salmali*
Bomba malabaricum

Description: This is a big tree. The leaves are 4 to 6 inches long, and tapering at the ends. The flowers are large and red in colour. The fruit is 6 to 7 inches long and ovoid. It is five valved and inside it are found silky material and many seeds. The bark contains thorns with a wide base. From the bark a resinous material comes out which is called *moca-rasa*. The root of a one or two-year-old tree is used as black musali.

Habitat: This tree grows wild in different parts of India, Sri Lanka, Indonesia and Malaysia. It is also planted on roadsides, parks and banks of ponds for its beautiful flowers.

Use in the reproductive system: The root of a young plant is used as an aphrodisiac. The resinous material secreted from the bark is used to prevent premature ejaculation and to promote the thickness of semen. It is nourishing and a promoter of virility. The immature green fruits are diuretic. The buds are used as a vegetable to promote sexual ability.

General use: The resinous extract and flowers are haemostatic. The paste of the bark cures burning sensations and oedema. The thorns of the bark are used externally in paste form to cure pimples and black pigmentation in the face and to promote complexion.

NUTMEG ✦ *Jatiphala*
Myristica fragrans

Description: The nutmeg tree is lofty with slender branches; elleptic-oblong leaves, pale yellowish-brown in colour. The flowers are 6 mm long and ellipsoid; the fruit is ovoid, 3.8 to 5 cm long.

Habitat: Nutmeg is cultivated in the Malay islands and peninsula. It grows in the east Moluccas and south India.

Use in the reproductive system: The fruit is bitter, hot and pungent. It is an aphrodisiac and is useful in diseases of the heart. It is also very useful in urinary discharges. The nut and the wall are diuretic, lactagogue and also act as a stimulant.

General use: Used generally as a carminative and antispasmodic, nutmeg is also useful in flatulence, nausea and vomiting. It is used in bronchitis, asthma and thirst. It also finds a place in culinary recipes.